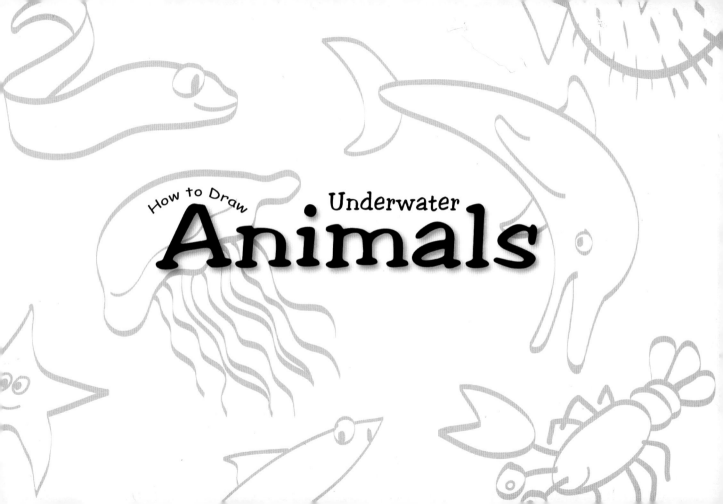

How to Draw Underwater Animals

For Jesse, Jasmine, Justin, Jordan, Melina, and Matthew

Published in the United States of America by The Child's World®
PO Box 326 • Chanhassen, MN 55317-0326
800-599-READ • www.childsworld.com

Acknowledgments
Illustration and Design: Rob Court
Production: The Creative Spark, San Juan Capistrano, CA

Registration

Library of Congress Cataloging-in-Publication Data
Court, Rob, 1956–
  How to draw underwater animals / by Rob Court.
      p. cm. — (Doodle books)
  ISBN-13: 978-1-59296-810-7 (library bound : alk. paper)
  ISBN-10: 1-59296-810-4 (library bound : alk. paper)
  1. Marine animals in art—Juvenile literature. 2. Drawing—Technique—Juvenile
literature. I. Title. II. Series.

NC781.C68 2007
743.6—dc22
                                                    2006031564

The Scribbles Institute™

How to Draw Underwater Animals

Animals

by Rob Court

Doodle BOOKS™

The Child's World®

fish

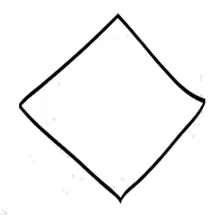

1

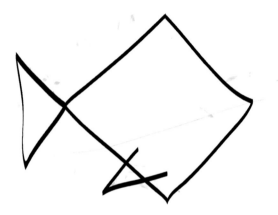

2

3

4

1

2

3

4

jellyfish

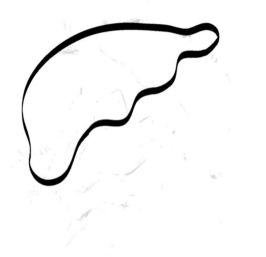

1

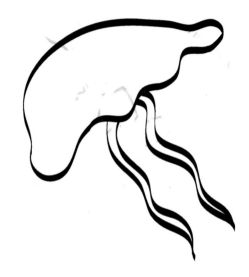

2

3

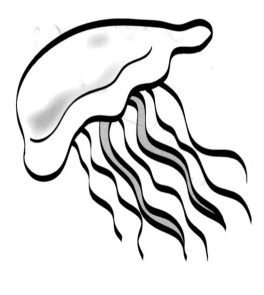

4

crab

1

2

3

4

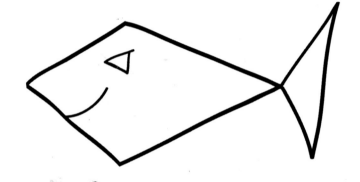

1

2

3

4

clam

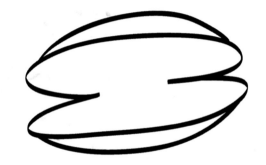

2

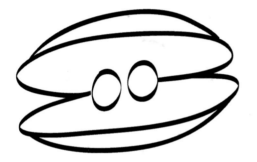

3

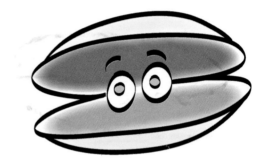

4

1

2

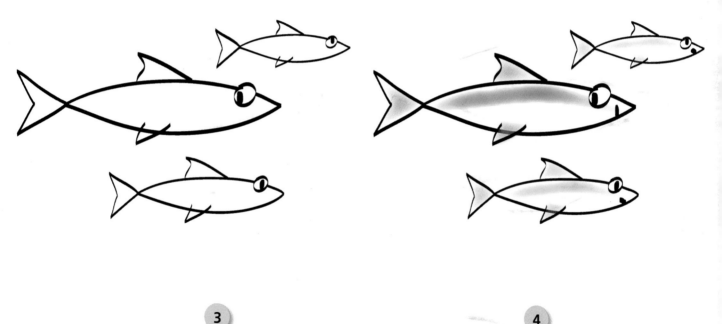

3

4

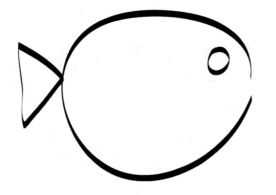

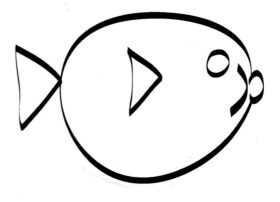

1

2

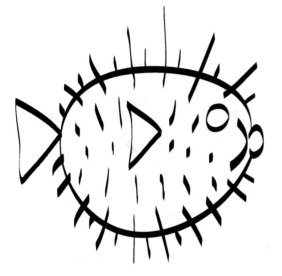

3

4

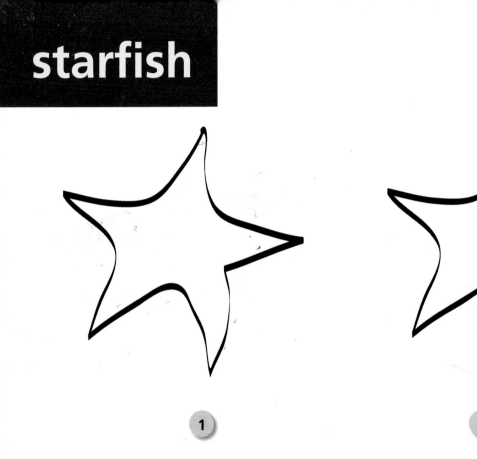

1

2

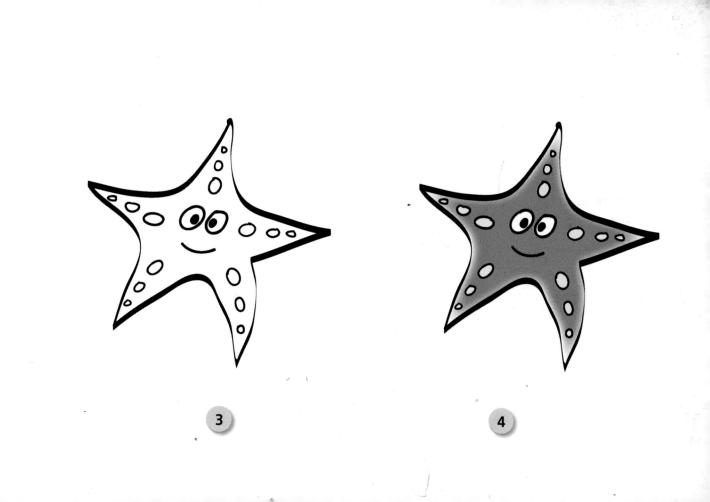

3

4

lobster

1

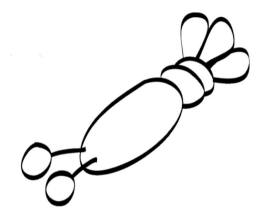

2

3

4

1

2

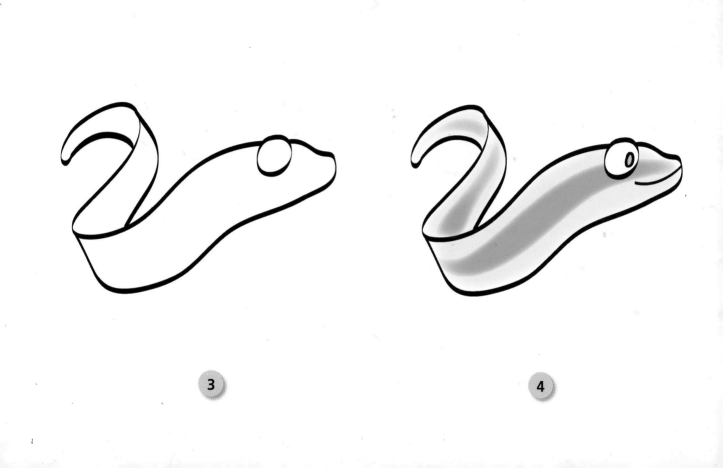

3

4

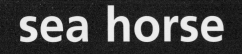

sea horse

1

3

4

dolphin

1

2

3

4

octopus

1

2

3

4

lines

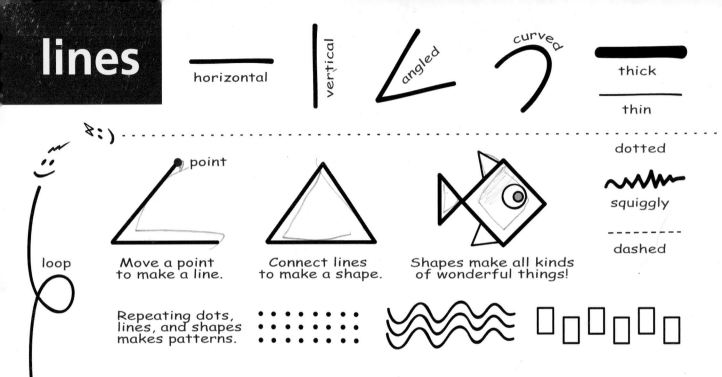

horizontal

vertical

angled

curved

thick

thin

dotted

squiggly

dashed

point

loop

Move a point to make a line.

Connect lines to make a shape.

Shapes make all kinds of wonderful things!

Repeating dots, lines, and shapes makes patterns.

About the Author

Rob Court is a graphic artist and illustrator. He started the Scribbles Institute to help students, parents, and teachers learn about drawing and visual art. Please visit www.scribblesinstitute.com